D0399865

DISCARD

MARY BURRITT CHRISTIANSEN POETRY SERIES
Hilda Raz, Series Editor

Mary Burritt
Christiansen
Poetry Series

The Mary Burritt Christiansen Poetry Series publishes two to four books a year that engage and give voice to the realities of living, working, and experiencing the West and the Border as places and as metaphors. The purpose of the series is to expand access to, and the audience for, quality poetry, both single volumes and anthologies, that can be used for general reading as well as in classrooms.

Also available in the University of New Mexico Press Mary Burritt Christiansen Poetry Series:

América invertida: An Anthology of Younger Uruguayan Poets
  edited by Jesse Lee Kercheval
Family Resemblances: Poems by Carrie Shipers
The Woman Who Married a Bear: Poems by Tiffany Midge
Self-Portrait with Spurs and Sulfur: Poems by Casey Thayer
Crossing Over: Poems by Priscilla Long
Heresies: Poems by Orlando Ricardo Menes
Report to the Department of the Interior: Poems by Diane Glancy
The Sky Is Shooting Blue Arrows: Poems by Glenna Luschei
A Selected History of Her Heart: Poems by Carole Simmons Oles
The Arranged Marriage: Poems by Jehanne Dubrow

For additional titles in the Mary Burritt Christiansen Poetry Series, please visit unmpress.com.

Untrussed *poems*

Christine Stewart-Nuñez

Farmington Public Library
2101 Farmington Avenue
Farmington, NM 87401

University of New Mexico Press ∞ Albuquerque

002000444374

© 2016 by Christine Stewart-Nuñez
All rights reserved. Published 2016
Printed in the United States of America
21 20 19 18 17 16   1 2 3 4 5 6

Library of Congress Cataloging-in-Publication Data

Names: Stewart-Nuñez, Christine, author.
Title: Untrussed : poems / Christine Stewart-Nuñez.
Description: Albuquerque : University of New Mexico Press, 2016. |
Series: Mary Burritt Christiansen Poetry Series
Identifiers: LCCN 2016000858 (print) | LCCN 2016004933 (ebook) |
ISBN 9780826357168 (softcover : acid-free paper) |
ISBN 9780826357175 (electronic)
Classification: LCC PS3619.T5353 A6 2016 (print) | LCC PS3619.T5353 (ebook) |
DDC 811/.6—dc23
LC record available at http://lccn.loc.gov/2016000858

Cover photograph courtesy of Lila Sanchez
Author photograph courtesy of Terrance Stewart
Designed by Lila Sanchez
Composed in Dante MT Std 11.5/13.5
Display type is Dante MT Std

for my Loves

I wish poetry were not read as autobiography, although of course, it draws all the materials of life. We have to contend with the idea of mortality; we all, at some point, love, with the risks involved, the vulnerabilities involved, the disappointments and great thrills of passion, so what you use is the *self as a laboratory* in which to practice, master, what seem to you central dilemmas.

—Louise Glück quoted by Grace Cavalieri in "The Poet and the Poem from the Library of Congress: Poets Laureate on Public Radio, 1977–2014"

Contents

I Wonder

about perspective; we finish
less what's farther away. Here's
a petal, flower, bush, garden;
there's a horizon of trees, landscape
framed east and west. I wonder

about distance. Izhvesk, islands,
Italy, India are close at hand;
Jupiter and Mercury diminish
in the heavens. I wonder about

shifts. Here's a cubed melon, bowl
of cream, mint leaf, spoon, cloth
napkin; there's the slant of light
that alters the color of the fruit's

flesh. I wonder how we can trust
what we see. Here's the spark
and there's the wind that fuels
it up—a ribbon of flame. I
wonder why everything dissolves

when we look away.

Wonder Woman Ponders the Kiss

A few years ago, Earth captured
Cruithne, an asteroid revolving
in an ellipse. That chunk of rock
slipped into orbit effortlessly, just
as he slid into their plot-altering embrace.
When today's newspaper reported
a third moon—space junk—Diana
waited until dawn, expecting the porch
to creak under his footsteps. Why
should he assume the universe fixed?
She searched for star luster, scanned
for unusual specks of light. With new
moon tomorrow, she won't wait
to know how his crescent-curved
body silhouettes her own.

Lovebirds

In Izhvesk, a once-closed city, factories anchor
the shoreline, churn sludge into a reservoir, blow

plumes of smoke from chimneys. Cigarettes
stick out of concrete blocks. The economy's core—

AK-47 of Kalashnikov's design,
hunting rifles, pistols—employs everyone.

Near the city square, a monument to industrial
soldiers: a bronze man fitted with boots,

pants wrapping chiseled thighs, arm
hoisting a flag. A wedding party poses there,

the bride's white cocktail dress against the groom's
black suit. Cameras click and vodka glasses clink.

Birds, fluffy white with black neckbands, ignore
the perpetual flame, metal-tinged air, couple's

sweaty sheen of wedding work; their claws
scratch along cement as they shuffle toward
each other, feathered breasts touching as they meet.

Miguel's Beach Paradise

Four days in, we dive, fold
our bodies, skirt reefs alongside
flicker fish, and slice seawater

with wide kicks. On a stretch
of coral, I pluck a conch
and nestle it in the crook

of my arm. By sunset, spring
water glistens on this ocean crown.
A calico cat rubs against

its ridges, a relief map
of the sea's history.
In the curve of the shell,

the cat hears waves. Where
Miguel had cut out a crescent
to harvest meat, the pink

whitens. We're served
grilled shrimp, pineapple
rum punch, lobster salad

with curried conch. As I roll
it over my tongue, press
it against my mouth's roof,

days replay: hours in the sea,
in our bed. With salt
on our skin, I listen for sighs;

we curl into each other
and surface.

Variation of Crane

As cranes descend, black ink seeping
from twilight onto the Platte River's
sandbars, I can't imagine defensive
kicks or pecks; birds glide and spill
onto this parchment of sand.

Moving calligraphy, my husband:
clad in black, brown belt doubled
in back, he walks across sky-blue
carpet—every muscle's flex
a flow as seamless as breath.

Where the river curves like the arch
of his bare foot, like the letters
he writes in the air when he moves—
a fossil: six-foot wingspan
and pointed beak. A sandhill crane.

Once, when we slept tangled
in crisp sheets, his arm looped,
a cursive flourish penned around
my neck. Choke hold. He woke,
amazed by my presence.

How do instincts, whether twenty
million years of practice or two
decades, train a body to such
vigilance? Even in dreams
we fight or fly or freeze.

On the mat, his right hand
is a fist at his waist; his hips turn
and knee bends. He lifts his left
foot to touch his inner thigh—
an alphabet for grace.

Into night, water, each other,
cranes settle. Feather colors
match the hues of corn husks
in nearby fields. Beaks scratch
survival in patches of snow.

Thump, thump ripples through
silence. Sinews and flock flash.
A pivot evades danger. These
signature moves can save us:
exhale and lift your wings.

The Stars Say Compatible

Taurus speaks the language
of flowers. She unpuzzles a stem's
backbend, iris petal as smooth as
a baby's cheek. Cancer carries ocean
under his tongue. On island time
he moves surf and stirs crushed shells.
He discovers her note: Shade lilies
bloom between us; surrender. Tidal,
he pulls with thoughts; succulents
become coral, butterflies visiting
her garden, angelfish. She twists
the honeymoon into hibiscus,
morning unfolded in velvet tips.
He remembers dolphins. Someday,
when he swims in kelp's embrace,
he'll see daisies. For her, silence
will smell like honey and salt.
When winds bathe the Plains,
they'll hear the sea, waves paced
like a sleeping child's breath.

Cycles

Curved glass, through the telescope's
metal arm, bent light and dropped

the moon so close I could almost
touch this seed dangling in the swath

of sky, its surface the color of cream—
an egg just burst through the galaxy's

fallopian tube, round and ready,
as I was, for the next step. He said

it wasn't the best time, the orb's fullness
too bright to see mountains and rills

in stark relief, craters where ancient
debris skidded across the surface.

Mares, he explained, were dry lava
beds. I'd remember that later

while he, stretched out on the bed,
studied pockmarked ceiling tiles

as I undressed, the shower's glass
transparent in the studio motel room.

Lathering soap from nose
to knee, I invited desire to eclipse

doubt and suspend him above me,
our bodies yoked and orbiting.

Sheer Communication

Odd intonations pin a veil between us;
an errant word a scrim of faille between us.

Diaphanous, like the moon's halo, this light
obscures dimensions when words fail between us.

We believe in fog, not cloud, a mist that lifts
and leaves us lost in the vale between us.

A gossamer on switch grass, ice laced above
a moving stream: a sentence stale between us.

One wall thins at a time until the tissue-
built city blurs, the moment pale between us.

Step back and we'll dissolve into filaments,
silence echoing on the trail between us.

Observations from the Hall

No key exists for the map of his mind's
highways. Before, if I held his body against
mine and rested my cheek beneath his jaw's
stubble, he'd speak. Before, if I slid my fingernail
from his hairline to shoulder, if my hand
molded against his bicep's hard muscle,
he'd begin a story. Grief has wormed in, dulled
his quick wit. Between a full-backed chair
and flickering screen, he hermits into lives
of brain-lusting zombies, men in capes
and caves. At 2 a.m., the computer's glow
caresses his thigh. He moves the mouse
from one pale-skinned, raven-haired character
to another as they sigh sorrow into his hungry ear.

The Holding

My weaving teacher—a man
who sells baskets the size
of a woman's womb filled
with baby, bowls in shapes
of slow cookers and skillets,
containers for mittens, mail,
maps—has wrinkles like grooves
of bark. In his hands, commitment
works willows as if they were
straws; in my nose, the scents
of rain and wood unfurl.
Branches like long, clasped
arms carpet the floor with color:
cocoa, rust, maple-leaf orange.

As a child, I hid behind
a pussy willow while my father
drank away the smell of bullets.
My mother distilled dreams
in daily bread. I plucked covers
from silken fluff before catkins
grew puffy, yellow fuzz tickling
my cheek. The next week, leaves
appeared as if change was easy,
two syllables vowed, words
braided into the fabric of living.

I pinch and bend supple
wood between layers whispering,
push, pull up, move through.
Sore with an hour's work, I
stumble. Gaps spring open even
as I account for the branches'
flex and flaws. Yet I trust these
woven rings, put in my husband's
hands, will bear the weight we need.

Wonder Woman Does Dream Dirty

She doesn't want to sound
like a god's daughter when
she cums. Her Greek slides
to the wayside, accent softening
DC style. Multiple is a series
of Os, not the syllables of sex talk.
Simple slang suits her: *cunt*
not *clitoris*, *blow* not *fellatio*.
She'll make love no matter
how you phrase it (*cream*,
grind, *vault*, *fiddle*) because
she's promised to rescue you
from evil's clutches, launder
your sweaty shorts, and polish
your medals for eternity. Just
don't request Paradise Island stories.
She'll whisper, Cock, tits, pussy,
ass as easy as, Change their minds
and change the world!
You might say, Good girls
don't talk like that. Good thing
she's not—it's the Amazon's
code to help anyone in need.
Look, the invisible jet's spotless,
serviced, fueled. You bring
the jizz. Wonder Woman's
always juiced to fly hot.

Peonies Framed by Sappho

Come, then, loose me from cruelties.
Frost, spring's morning lace, no

longer endangers. Ants unfurl
buds under a sheet of fog. Feet

pry and press until petals burst:
red, pink—double crowns—scent

released from the core's fist.
Unsealed blossoms flop over

fences. I cut seven crimson,
two blush. Five white even

out the bouquet's number.
Peonies spread, scent the whole

house with June. One flower
drapes—an umbrella; ants spill

down the vase. To my bare feet,
shears slip. Save me. Peel away

doubt with tender friction—
give my tethered heart its full desire.

Polish Lessons

Through hard Cs, Vs, Zs—sounds
of rakes through dirt, a spade's thwack
into clay—blended letters take root.
As translucent slices, beets blush
in borsht; these whorl-etched coins
our table's underworld evidence
of bloodlines, planted words. Air
sucked between teeth becomes
a buzz of swarming bees, the breeze
through lilacs in Stryszów, ghost bullets
zipping through air, a mother's *hush-
baby-hush*. When I form the syllables
of *kawa białe* and sip its rich cream, I fall
not for sugar melting into dark brew
but for the way round, rollicking vowels
lasso my tongue and open up my mouth.

First Bases

If Mae West was right—a man's kiss
is his signature—then sign on again
across the faded ink of the first fool
to fall for my smile, the haunted-house

smooch starting in a rickety car, Scott's
hand snaking up my shirt, my lips
parting after a peck. Let's mimic Rodin's
lovers in *The Kiss*; I'll throw my arm

over your neck, your hand at my waist.
Morning won't send this again: child
asleep, quiet house holding its breath
against cold autumn winds. I was two

years old when I first pursed and closed
my eyes, a neighbor's house framing
the photo of my lips pressed to a red tulip.
When I hold stems again, a bundle

of nodding bells, I recall the soft palm
of a hand that drew me in for an unrequited
kiss—he a former student. I should've
let our lips brush, kissed off my conscience.

Now I just smack your lips and skim
skinned knees when our boy falls.
When I sleep alone, I recall your hand
cupping my cheek, the house spinning

as we stood dizzy in our first kiss.
Sweetheart, let's find that blazing space
again—what we named love—
and seal it hand to hand, lip to lip.

Panning for Pearls

When life flies
in impossible
lanes, she picks
up his boxers
off the floor
and the phone rings
dahlias, petals
dropping out
of the air at the shrill
tone's end.
When he fills
the car with gas,
her book smells
like cinnamon
buns, sugary,
dog-eared corners
flaking off.
He swirls
thunderstorms
in his hand during
commercials
and lightning
illuminates his
palm's lines; rain
puddles in the creases
of hers. Can two
kiss from the same
cup? The TV's
white noise
coats the wall
with Styrofoam
popcorn and each
window along
the whitewash
frames the moon.
On Fridays with
enough light,
they lean in.

A Photograph Suggests Depression

When he sulks in a midsummer slump, I analyze
a photo of winter, its edges of gray scale: pristine

snow dulled by lead-white lighting. The sky beyond
the tallest black branches? Silver, suggesting sun

behind monochromatic clouds. Otherwise, the flat
sheath of snow marks an axis: horizontal sidewalk,

park benches, long-stretch fence; vertical street lamps,
tree trunks. If we stepped off the curb, I'd smell exhaust

in the crisp city air; he would walk into stillness.
Instead, wind has blown itself away. Snow cleaves

to bark. How easily it could flake off, crystals
winking one last time. How simple the solution

if it meant sunshine stretching through, my hand
touching his elbow. Branches rise up and shoot

off, diagonal at the photo's top, the forking lines
resembling networks, imbalanced neurons

sparking against the dark backdrop of bone.

Fifth of July

For five nights, fireworks
have burst into orchids—
red, white, and blue stamens
sizzling every seven
seconds against the black
blanket of sky. Outside
the bedroom window, smoke
tendrils kiss the Dipper
and orange-hued orb. Do I
still stir you? Tomorrow,
firecracker confetti
will stick to snapdragons,
a neighbor's origami
orgy gone awry. Charcoal
snakes will scar sidewalks
and sparklers will spike lawns.
Bottle rockets—purple, frayed—
will stand for one more try
inside empty Coors cans.
Forget the cookout's burgers
and egg salad, the parade
of bands and bike-riding Shriners,
the sweets filling candy bags.
Our first Independence Day,
sprays of light crossed and
recrossed the sky. Summer's
simmer might stretch across
the year, but do you miss
the hot nights you searched for
a new wick, a fresh match?

Each Night, His Other Life

Into his toon body—penciled
biceps bulging, jeans filled
with thick-as-tree-trunk thighs—
her husband morphs at midnight.

Issues of *The Punisher*
and classic *Spider-Man* litter
the hardwood floors, relieved
of their protective sleeves.

Wham! Pow! When balloons
of dialog float on their bedroom
walls, he prepares to leave,
tiptoeing past his son who dreams

of little llamas, grouchy lady-
bugs, Chihuahuas, and candy
canes. She composes the bed's
blank page. Dagger-edged,

sleek, he walks Main: his shadow
startles a drunk—keys fall down,
lost at the car door; a light
lit foils a man casing a silent

house. Sunrise. He slips into bed:
cheek scarred, shirt smeared,
foot creased. Who needs a double
life? Gloss leaves his lips supple,

muffling his story. She's tired
and her version's inked in red,
so she caresses his clothed
arm, pulling sheets over them both.

Unintended Consequences

Tug off your shadow, gray
scrim over skin; I'll see your roots,
study what grows in darkness, and weigh
the cost of seeking too many routes

to your heart. In time, new shoots
will sprout even if you pray
otherwise. Branches yield fruits
we can't imagine. How will this day

end for us? Green-flecked soil. Stray
seeds fly across the sky. What suits
you is the sun's bloom. Will I pay
the cost of seeking too many routes?

Wind-Shifted City

Phoenix, you were like a lover
I didn't love. At first, I adored
the dry heat, a throaty voice

radiating innuendo. Rolled Rs
seduced me. Daily sky service—
sun in cloudless blue, a hue

just shy of ice—bleached
clean my need for water.
Winter's green lichen speckled

on rocks seemed enough.
I ignored ivory houses,
the hum of traffic melting

on freeways. Sunscreen-
doused transplants flooding
plots of crabgrass didn't

inspire a sip from the tap.
During monsoons, moonless
horizons comforted me.

Used to hot breath on my neck
and a cuff of wind around my wrist,
I expected to say, I do.

A breeze played flower girl,
sprayed cement with blossoms
twice a snowflake's size,

made semen-scented streets.
When the temperature spiked
to one hundred degrees four

hours beyond sunrise and smog
thickened around my neck,
the message salted my tongue:

leave, leave, or settle for thirst.

Wonder Woman Relaxes

Closing her steno pad at five, Diana
contemplates cuisine, not the break
room's lime JELL-O. Superfood:

spinach sautéed in olive oil, quinoa
pilaf with Turkish apricots. Once
home (glasses off, hair ponytailed,

sweatpants on) she slices a pineapple
like it's cream cheese. As she juliennes
jalapeños, she needs no magic bracelet;

golden lassos won't quicken the task.
She admires the cut's discernment.
When her man's in trouble, Wonder

Woman busts him out; slaps, slugs,
strikes, what does it matter if she
breaks a nail or three? Her man

doesn't see her. Post-mission, he's
safe watching TV, and Diana's free
to pummel villains with Superman,

Aquaman. They love her feminine
touch. Tonight, comics will wait.
Skimming across the dusty wine

rack, she chooses a Cab, Opus One,
'85, and pulls out the company,
crème brûlée. On the balcony, she

dines, the city's honks and calls
her symphony. Sirens pulse
through her veins like a heartbeat.

We Were Full, Once

Tuscan raindrops tasted buttery sliding from May
skies, and those spilling onto Florentine streets
seemed artful as if clouds in Milan had designed
them in the spirit of Brunelleschi and Donatello;
they resembled water balloons, nipple-less
breasts, avant-garde vases, Anjou pears. Buoyant,
those raindrops, as if conceived in Reims, sons
of champagne bubbling over Lyon and Nice
before splashing down on us, drunk on *David*
and *La Primavera*. Flattened against storefront
windows, no end in sight, we ducked into a café
to nibble chocolate, sip cappuccinos. Sunshine
embellishing our table in ochre light drew us back
onto cobblestone, water gleaming on stained glass,
gilded churches flinging doors open as we passed.

Complementary in Theory

Juxtapose hues of white—as this diamond
shows—to see relief. Inside, an isabel
layer, square of antiflash, rectangle of blonde.
Opposite colors blend to create a neutral

as this palette implies. The artist's parallel
areas divided with a thin, black column.
Below midpoint, two triangles of eggshell
speak subtlety. A line of linen and bone band

are slight shifts. As with a blizzard's horizon,
a bichon frise, baby's breath, a blank cell,
we limit vision if we insist on what's common—
opposite colors blend to create a neutral.

Storm Sex Remembered

At a blizzard's beginning
I watched snowflakes pirouette,
wind choreographing an arc—
left, left—before they turned,
schools of snow fish dancing.

As drifts piled up, foot by foot,
I heard the sound before
language; a whisper between
falling flakes became a sigh
against the silk of neck, ribs.

As it intensified, street lamps
glowed under a gauze of snow.
Wind whined through panes,
glass frosting over with lace maps
that melted from our skin's heat.

As I pulled his breath
into me, my body hummed
with the energy of stars.
Such icy fire. With his hand
on my hip, I wept.

Clarity

The types of eyes that grow
in Taos: those the color of gray-blue
clouds settled among the Sangre
de Cristo peaks, the distant range
an arm wrapped around the town;
eyes that pierce wispy silver-white
strati hovering above New Mexico's
luminous skin and that pan across
the landscape of Russian olive trees,
thorns spiked in a distant dirt; eyes
the temperature of desert adobe
and the texture of metallic shrubs;
those with lashes of birds twittering
under a nude sun; those that flash
like the sheen of the stumbling dog's
coat and that wrinkle like marigolds;
eyes that see my husband, fifteen
hundred miles away, who doesn't miss
my foot against his own.

A Study of Perception

Banana, yolk, daffodil: the sun peaks at yellow
so human eyes and our star are in sync at yellow.

Triplets of the primary world: red, blue, green;
why not citrine, straw? The baby speaks at yellow.

Cones, rods, retinas differ, yet we calibrate hues
of black-eyed Susans blooming this week at yellow.

If someone blind kissed my eyelids, I'd discern *school
bus* from *daisy field*. Please start the critique at yellow.

Color's a union of surface and light—a marriage
begun with the sun's turn, oblique at yellow.

I wanted to be that gold square, butterscotch lozenge,
un cadeau sans bow. My longing piqued at yellow.

Muscle Memory

Tonight he says we're too much
work. I recall the piano-lesson stint,
drunken-rhythm melodies lurching
out of the upright as his fingers
searched for keys, as he plunked out
crossovers, as he squinted at *Easy
Piano for Adults*. He untangled a mess
with his mnemonic: Every Good
Boy Does Fine. I remember how

Good Eats played over and over until
he knew the angel food cake recipe
by heart. After dozens of eggs were
cracked and separated, whites hand-
mixed for seven minutes, and cakes
baked until browned, he trashed
two—they tasted delicious but
the texture wasn't right. I think

back to that Santa Monica beach
where he practiced cane-fighting
for hours. His arms whistled through
the air, stick-turned-bone-breaker
kicking up sand. He transformed
that stealth weapon. Closet-bound,
it gathers dust. I gave up learning

to play by ear. As he moves beyond
the scope of my arms, my muscles
know only to cling.

Breakup Nonce

Blood comes after *blond*
in *Webster's*. Backbite—

not nibbling beetles
on a balsa-wood bench

but his behavior in bed
after the binge. She

brabbled about Barolo
and belugas; he believed

the second-brightest beta
was a fish. Six crystal

bells, cracked: belladonna
berries brightened under

them once. Beg broken
bits in a bundle of batiste.

Bergamot is a pear-shaped
orange; bezel the bijou's

side, the one lost while
weeding beets. Baba:

father and rum-soaked
cake. Baby-blue eyes:

her name and an herb.
Belay—obtain a hold—

belated advice. What
comes before *blood*?

A Palette of Turns

Early on, there were subtle turns:
a turn of the shoulder followed
by three steps out of the room, a turn
of phrase that cast sarcasm across
the car, a turn of mumbled replies
into silence, an outstretched hand
turned back.

After missing three lessons, that
Friday's date night we learned to cook
Chinese food, laughing and licking
our spoons clean. After missing parades
and picnics, that Saturday we picked
apples with the kid, and the autumn
breeze ushered in a buoyancy:

We're turning this relationship around.

I soaked up the scene: his saunter
down the dirt path, basket in hand;
the kid on his shoulders giggling
as he reached up through the leaves
to pick the fruit; our arms heavy
with bounty; the apples' blushed skin.

I saw only what I wanted to see,
and he performed perfectly—perhaps
inspired by nostalgia or sentiment.
That night when he said divorce
out loud, I knew his heart had already,
long ago, made the turn.

Abecedarian to Unbind

Zygal: H-formed as in
yokes, unions. Ours
xanthic against a rusty
wall and ten rungs tall, the
very ladder of our decade.
Untether that wood, your word.
Take back better, worse,
sickness, health.
Remove the ring. I won't ask
questions: why, who, when.
Pick necessities: enamel dutch
oven, Miyazaki films,
New York photos. And step down.
May you descend
leaving no marks. We both
know love's eclipsed by rotted
joints, that misaligned angles
interfere with anniversaries.
Honor the splinters, ache of
gradual ascent, the view, just
forget the full circle unless
end means beginning. I release
dusk's hot promises. Seek
clarity; you're no longer my
breath. May these lines
ax, split, divide, annul. Amen.

Wonder Woman's Amnesia

She doesn't react to the bite
of lemons, tart on her tongue;
prickly pear blushing magenta
among copper-streaked rock
ridges; the temperature
of winter's needled breath;
the image of a sun dog's luminous
rings; the smells of blackberries,
cedar, fungus. Yet she hears
the bonfire snap air ripe
with rain, sees a halo of wings
above the flames, feels the wind
caressing her shorn locks.
Diana, resist the urge to crawl
beneath the bell jar of oak, scoop
cool soil into your mouth, curl
your toes around roots; trust
that you'll know what to do.

Surprises of the Taj Mahal

She felt frost turn to mist
in an open-air rickshaw in Agra,
predawn. He held his rough
cheek against hers. She mused,
This monument to love is a tomb?
Not a palace? Not a place designed
for living? At sunrise, he spotted
the foundation for the king's
version, never built. The buried
queen died giving birth to her
fourteenth child, a daughter,
who lived a long life. Behind
white alabaster, a guide flashed
a light, and the flowers of inlaid
malachite, lapis lazuli, and agate
shimmered. The king planned twin
tombs, he said, shock lifting his
voice. His story of their end?
An epic next to her sparse lines.
A woman in hijab sitting
beside the reflecting pool, back
to the sun—her surviving photo.

After It's Over

Narrow grooves reveal texture
the artist's strokes of liquid pigment
resisted. Color applied with feather-
fine points split the print—one segment

now three. With orange I washed his print
away; it reappears at times, a gesture
of the body's habit. When his eyes hint
anger, I blink red and feel no pleasure.

In the frame, blue plumes measure
space between swaths of rust, a figment
of change. Which hue responds to pressure?
Fine points split a life, mark one segment.

Caravan Souvenir

It took months to name
the refraction, an illusion

composed in air. Leather
reins scraped the ground

and snorting, stamping
camels distracted me from

the hovering mirage. On
Thar's dunes, heat phased

out the full moon until
twilight surrendered to noon.

Just as it sucked breath
from our lungs, the desert

promised satisfaction. Beneath
a greening *khejri*, I ate curry

so hot fire bloomed
in my belly. My addiction

to honey-sweetened loaves
and meat seasoned with

cloves, cardamom, and ginger
was not yet complete; he

obsessed over creosote
and a blanket of lavender fog

thrown over a mountain's back.
I returned to a campfire

extinguished, saved a handful
of ash. Filtered by dust,

stars burned for rain. Only
we forgot to yearn.

Women Defending Castle with Bow and Crossbow

Only posies? Without arrows—
just flowers—I wonder.
One at the barbican stows
a posy between her thumb and finger;
a crossbow, aimed from the apse,
is empty. Midway, a woman steadies
a blossom with her hand, another grasps
a bunch by the stems, ready
to fling them over the parapet.
Even gold petals adorn
the red background. Some interpret
this as *a woman's greatest weapon
is love*. But once a heart's deployed
to battle, one can't call it back to bed.

We Pour So Much into the Making

—Toledo's Glass Pavilion

In this pavilion's panes, sheer
material folds like scrolls
of light and walls compress air.
Invisible pressure. Surfaces
reflect trees, the gauzy outlines
of patrons, sunlight constellating
on square tiles. Glass begins
as flint, sand, or spar—a silicious
substance fused with a flux:
soda, sea salt, wood ash.
Artisans vitrify frit and convert
clay over crucibles of heat
to create transparent sheets
from pearl ash, a word that only
sounds like ocean dust. Even
the architect knows panes
can fracture. Glass is fluid
liquid. Centuries reverse
perfect fusions, fired earth
becoming puddles of sand.

Struck

I assumed fire was the tallgrass prairie's
terror, flames sweeping six hundred feet
per minute, any rare seed-born flower lost.
I assumed romance was cultivated
at play on the storming skin of Earth,
metal key at the kite's end. I assumed
fifty million bison grazed gold waves
eight feet tall in peace. Now I know

Dakota, how dozens of zigzagged bolts
light up big bluestem, Indian grass, prairie
cordgrass to turn a summer dusk
into day. Now I know perennial forbs
survive as tubers, switch grass renewing
from the stem, not the blade's tip. Now
I know what's worth such stampedes
of heat: shoots dotting acres of ash.

Collecting Cocoons and Weaving Silk

Stranger, if you collected me now under the bright
South Dakota stars, if you opened the door
of my suburban chrysalis, you'd find me digesting
myself. The protein-rich ooze of the pupa stage
looks like books in boxes, empty frames leaning
against a wall, naked shelves, mounds of clothes
to pack, recycle, trash. Furniture-free, I've dumped
my guts. Dissect this, please. Find the spiral shell,
skillet, sapphire ring, jewel box, teddy bear, my life's
imaginal discs—stem cells to create black wings
and antennae. Soon, I'll moisten the windows
and push out. As much as I want to forget blue notes
and yellow flags, splotches of sky and touches of maize
will mark my flight. And I'll always be averse to the scent
of his house mark, even past the point of eclosion.

.

Wonder Woman Shops at the A&P

To satisfy her radiant-orange
appetite, Diana collects jars
of marmalade with crystallized
peels suspended in sugar, frozen
cylinders of citrus, two pounds
of organic carrots, a pumpkin.
Click-click, click-click, her scarlet
boots tap tiles as she grabs
packages with scents that hint:
ginger, juices, salmon, steak.
Her cart flashes with boxes
of orange pekoe, tangerines,
a sack of yams, apricots rolling
about, chunks of cheddar
and colby, peaches, peppers
the color of koi. At an aisle's end,
her bracelets clink against cool
glass as she selects sunflowers
for her table, their goldenrod
bonnets the texture of night.

Evolution

Dinosaur, I have fallen for your tyrant lizard
ways. Lording over triceratops and stegosaurus
on the toy table, you strike fear into Darth Vader's

heart. Han Solo escapes, but Skywalker screams
inside your pink-painted mouth, your jaw
unhinged, even as a toddler hugs your plastic

back, tugs your graceful tail's forty vertebrae.
Tyrannosaurus rex—last land dinosaur alive
before asteroids fell, before volcanoes spewed

liquid heat, before ash veiled Earth in darkness—
I love you not because of your twelve-inch teeth,
your seven-ton, ground-quaking step—a heft

inspiring chills in the Cretaceous Period's bravest
hadrosaurs—but because you're misunderstood.
Paleontologists lowered your top speed

by thirty-two kilometers; over conference tables
they slam down research, come to blows.
Some say you were black bodied, redheaded,

that your stink scared competitors away.
Others mourn their predator-king, ignoring
the nobility of those who do what their bodies

do best, be it three-toed theropod feet
or forelimbs of cortical bone. Does it matter
if you held your prey immobile? If binocular

vision and large olfactory bulbs mean
you fed on the nearly—or already—dead?
Under your smooth skin, the corded muscle,

some of your bones were too hollow to hold
your weight but are hallowed to humans
who study the story of your end. Do they see

you, my dearest *T. rex*, in the Andean condor?
Black feathers spanning eleven feet and soaring,
even at twenty-six pounds, to dine on whale,

llama, alpaca? How time limits us; if only we
evolved like you. Instead we wait for that spark
of surety, for our gods to give us wings.

New Delhi Fitting

When I duck behind
the screen, I submit
to the tailor's grace

with tape and numbers.
She measures lines
and curves; plump

or lean, her pleasure's
the same. Touching
waists and shoulders,

she speaks texture
and color, language
eclipsing my skin's

marks. She binds me
with silk, bold orange
and holly green, her oath

a gold-threaded hem.
Sari wrapped and spell
snug, I transform:

a sandalwood-carved
goddess, a moon of mango
sorbet, a bougainvillea
bouquet.

Crush

Is it *literary radical*, Pushkin, that pulls me past
Victorian commonplaces—blushing girls, blouses
back-buttoned from waist to hairline, lust bottled

with hyacinth and honeysuckle? Or is it your ubiquity
on these Moscow streets, the gaze of your sculpted
eyes a hand on my shoulder as I stroll? Your whispered

words stirred me before I viewed Kiprensky's
portrait of you in the Tretyakov: halo of curls, clear
hazel eyes, expression of alert concern as if

for me. Now, with this museum guard chirping
in my face (she must resent the way I bat my eyes
at the bust of you), I see how far I've fallen.

I use my own poems to fan heat rising in my thighs
when I see the columnar strength of your penmanship.
Cross-outs of words, phrases, lines—entire stanzas dizzy me.

If I close my eyes and touch the glass, I smell
ink and vellum, sweat on your brow. These words
I didn't recognize at first—the p's pronounced

as r's, b's as v's, consonants long, dripping songs
from strangers' lips. After studying silhouettes of men
in derbies and top hats, frock coats and trousers sketched

in margins, I swoon. Would you still thrill to see
illuminated copies of poems passed from hand to hand?
Darling, each day Russians resurrect you

in calques you created to expand the language.
By the time I see your death mask, I'm one
of the women in ballroom gowns whose elegant necks

you outlined, and I recall us dancing a quadrille—
exchanging pleasantries at first—then remembering
the Decembrist Revolt. Your bronze arm across

my shoulder flexes; do you recognize me?
I must have felt your temper flare when I heard
of Natalya's affair, must have felt the bullet pierce

when I heard of the duel, for even this simple
proximity to your pen makes me wistful for exile,
makes me curl up at your feet and write until I sleep.

Christine de Pisan, Writing

In my dream, I strolled through a City of Ladies
nude. Bricks were not women, our backs not
foundation (when I stopped my bare feet curved
over cobblestones). Instead, we populated
the public square: silk mercers sold cloaks;
the grace wife and her *accoucheuse* cooed
over a newborn; a lavender and limner
crossed an alley arm in arm; blowers,
brewsters, bunters, and buskers shared a pot
of tea. At first, I didn't recognize Artemisia
as a sempster when I peered into a boutique,
nor did I know Dido as a glazier when I glanced
into an artisan's stall. Yet there they were—
Blanche, Medea, Fredegund, Lecretia, Thisbe,
Sappho—disguised. When I found Christine
de Pisan in her studio, between a hatter's
and hand flowerer's, I expected her changed,
perhaps revealed as I was. But no.
Her Burgundian caul's horns pointed up,
hair covered in a white wimple; her royal-blue
dress accented her pale skin. I heard
the goose-feather quill scratching on vellum,
smelled the metallic scent of ink.
She looked up at me, put an eraser
into my hand and said, Your turn.

The Artist Paints the Sunset

She faces fire where colors coalesce,
heat an egg-yolk scarf she'll wear
in the lush moment just before ripeness.

She paints from her body, breath a caress
spreading indigo into the air.
She faces fire where colors coalesce

and sings boy-blanket blue across
the ceiling of this framed world. She'll dare
in the lush moment just before ripeness

and, with redbrick lipstick, press
her mouth into the sun's arc. She'll swear
she faces fire where colors coalesce,

speaking grapefruit light to bless
the clouds, textures blurring joy and despair
in the lush moment just before ripeness.

Full is her fire is her thought is her promise
as she unwinds paint from brush until bare.
She faces fire where colors coalesce
in this moment just before ripeness.

Beginning

I've emerged. Not from a painted grid
of orange and black strokes, distinct lines
and angles measured in inches, but hatched
from a shell, a bulb, a grain of salt, hatched
from that last life. Here's a new grid,
a fresh space: the crisscrossed lines
that mark my lover's skin. This grid
traces the blade's point, crack of a hatched
plan. My words press against these lines,
the lines of a mind hatched into the brush's grid.

Bodhisattva of the Kitchen Sink

In the brightening kitchen, she pulls
a dull-haired mop like a child
pressing a pencil top across gray-lined
paper, and she picks off a cushion's lint
like a robin worming for breakfast.
In arcs she scours shower stalls
as a carpenter sands off stain. What bliss
plays on her lips when her feather duster
tickles a desk, when her rag caresses
Grandma's pink Depression glass—
a cake plate—until it shines.

O Enlightened One, what lovers of fresh
scents do to woo you: sweep floors, dry
dishes, defrost refrigerators, polish
chandeliers. We invent vacuums
and self-cleaning ovens. Someone even
washed clothes, ironed shirts,
and folded brassieres. We ignore
the labor of elbow grease that birthed
you and forget how the teasing
of dust bunnies from under beds
demonstrates your devotion.

Love's in the press of palm to polish
trim, in a wrist's quick swipe
of toast crumbs, in circles that free
mirrors of streaks, in scratches
that unstick grit from textured walls.
Goddess of All Things Sparkling,
your pure heart pumps bleach.
Inspire my simple gestures; bestow
a kiss of cleanliness on me.

For Elizabeth, Who Loved to Square Dance

I wore Grandma Liz's pearls
for play, a plastic strand long
enough to pool on the carpet
over my stubbed toes. When I pull
them over my head now, I smell
phantoms: cigarettes, Estée
Lauder. I don't smoke or spritz
on perfume. I don't layer polyester
or perm my hair. I've slipped off
my wedding ring as she did, signed
divorce. What advice would she offer
for life between husbands? *Wear red
lipstick and always leave it behind.*

Acknowledgments

These poems, sometimes with different titles, appeared in the following periodicals:

Adanna Literary Journal: "Cycles"
Atlanta Review: "We Were Full, Once"
burntdistrict: "Struck" and "Wind-Shifted City"
Cherry Tree: A National Literary Journal @ Washington College: "Sheer Communication" and "Women Defending Castle with Bow and Crossbow"
Cider Press Review: "We Pour So Much into the Making"
Cimarron Review: "First Bases"
Clackamas Literary Review: "Lovebirds"
Connecticut Review: "A Photograph Suggests Depression" and "The Artist Paints the Sunset"
Crab Orchard Review: "Variation of Crane"
Flyway: Journal of Writing and the Environment: "Miguel's Beach Paradise"
Fox Cry Review: "Bodhisattva of the Kitchen Sink"
Louisiana Review: "Muscle Memory"
Natural Bridge: "Crush"
Paddlefish: "Polish Lessons" and "Wonder Woman's Amnesia"
Portland Review: "Abecedarian to Unbind"
Prairie Schooner: "The Stars Say Compatible"
Sheepshead Review: "The Holding"
Sierra Nevada Review: "For Elizabeth, Who Loved to Square Dance" and "Wonder Woman Shops at the A&P"
South Dakota Review: "Observations from the Hall," "Panning for Pearls," and "Wonder Woman Ponders the Kiss."

"A Study of Perception" and "Beginning" were included in *Memory, Echo, Words* edited by Norma C. Wilson (Scurfpea Publishing, 2014)

"Caravan Souvenir," "Clarity," "Miguel's Beach Paradise," "Peonies Framed by Sappho," "Polish Lessons," "The Stars Say Compatible," "Storm Sex Remembered," "Wonder Woman Ponders the Kiss," and "Wonder Woman's Amnesia" were included in the chapbook *Snow, Salt, Honey: Ten Poems* by Christine Stewart-Nuñez (Red Dragonfly Press, 2012)

"Each Night, His Other Life" and "Wonder Woman Relaxes" were included in *Drawn to Marvel: Poems from the Comic Books* edited by Bryan D. Dietrich and Marta Ferguson (Minor Arcana Press, 2014)

I wish to thank the many people who gave me feedback and encouragement on these poems, including Darla Biel, Gary Dop, Jeanne Emmons, Rochelle Harris, Susan Kan, Scott King, Erika Stevens, and Joy Zarzana. My gratitude to the following entities for gifts of time and financial support: South Dakota Art Museum Fellowship Program, South Dakota State University College of Arts and Sciences (Griffith Grant), South Dakota State University's Academic and Scholarly Excellence Initiative/Research Support, South Dakota State University Department of English, and the Kimmel Harding Nelson Center for the Arts. My deepest thanks to Hilda Raz, editor of the Mary Burritt Christiansen Poetry Series, and Elise McHugh, senior acquisitions editor at the University of New Mexico Press, for selecting this book for publication. Finally, with appreciation and love to my parents, brother, and friends for their unwavering support; with thanks and love to Holden, my son and hero, who has taught me more about what it means to love in nine years than anyone ever could; and with gratitude and love to Brian for his courage to build a new life with me.

Notes on References and Ekphrasis

The book's epigraph by Louise Glück was found in Grace Cavalieri's "The Poet and the Poem from the Library of Congress: Poets Laureate on Public Radio, 1977–2014" published in the *Writer's Chronicle* (February 2015).

"Sheer Communication"
After *Rooftops of Barcelona* by Madeline Ritz, South Dakota Art Museum.

"Peonies Framed by Sappho"
The first and last lines are attributed to Sappho.

"Unintended Consequences"
After *Propagations* by Susan Heggestad, South Dakota Art Museum.

"Complementary in Theory"
After *White Diamond* by Ilya Bolotowsky, Cockerline Collection, South Dakota Art Museum.

"A Study of Perception"
After *Yellow Square* by Ilya Bolotowsky, Cockerline Collection, South Dakota Art Museum.

"After It's Over"
After *Season of Change* by Cynthia Reeves, South Dakota Art Museum.

"Women Defending Castle with Bow and Crossbow"
After an illuminated manuscript of the same name by Walter de Milemete, English, 1326–1327, London, British Library. The italicized quote is taken from an informal online discussion of the piece.

"Collecting Cocoons and Weaving Silk"
After an illuminated manuscript by an unknown author, French, fifteenth century, London, British Library.

"Christine de Pisan, Writing"
After an illuminated manuscript of Christine de Pisan writing in her study, ca. 1410, London, British Library.

"The Artist Paints the Sunset"
After *Lush Moment Just Before Ripeness* by Betty L. Beer. Beer borrowed the
   phrase "lush moment just before ripeness" from Marlena De Blasi's
   book *A Thousand Days in Venice*.

"Beginning"
After *Hatch* by Beverly Pepper, South Dakota Art Museum.